Alphabet ABCDEFG
Number 012345
& Color ⟳⟳⟳⟳⟳
Poetry

A Fun, Learning Experience for All Students

Written and Illustrated by

Linda Taylor

Alphabet Color and Number Poetry by Linda Taylor

Copyright ©2010, 2019 Linda Taylor

All rights reserved. No part of this book may be reproduced or transmitted in any form or by any means, electronic or mechanical, including photocopying, recording, or by any information storage and retrieval system without permission in writing from the copyright owner.

ISBN: 978-1-947829-90-9

For Worldwide Distribution

Printed in the U.S.A.

Touch Point Productions & Publishing
Long Island, NY

Please visit our website: amazingannabelle.com

For children everywhere.

—L.T.

The Alphabet

ALPHABET

Letters we have learned
since we were two,
Sung countless times.
We love the breakthrough
When a child learns the alphabet
for the very first time.

We smile, we cheer,
Even shed a tear.
You see what happens
when you persevere!

Then you learn to write the alphabet
all kinds of ways.
We're so amazed,
We give you praise!
All hands are raised.

You're learning new things
and growing your wings.
You're flying through the ALPHABET!

Aa

A makes 2 sounds:
ă and ā,
ă for apple
ā for play.

Ă for alligator, cat,
and hat,
ā for today.
Everything's okay.

Aa

Bb

Bb is basketball,
bowling, and bait.
Bb is for bumblebee
buzzing near my plate.

Bb is for black.
Bb is for blue.
Bb is for a bouncing bear
bellowing yahoo!

Bb

Cc

Cc makes 2 sounds:
c and s,
c sound for candy
s sound for celery.

C sound for cupcakes
colorful and sweet.
S sound for celebrate,
cellar, and receipt.

Cc

Dd

Dd is for donuts,
dolls, and dough.
Dd is for dancing
do-si-do.

Dd is for doing,
so don't give up.
Dd is for dog
and his dear little pup.

Ee

Ee makes 2 sounds:
ĕ and ē,
ĕ for elephant
ē for eat.

Ĕ for echo, egg,
and met.
Ē for eel, electricity,
and feel.

Ff

Ff is for fish
swimming in a lake.
Ff is for a female fox
eating a few cakes.

Ff is for a funny face,
so act like me.
We'll make a frown just like a clown
and frolic happily.

Ff

Gg

Gg makes 2 sounds:
g and j,
g sound for girl
j sound for giraffe.

G sound for go,
gum, and gay.
J sound for gym, and
the giant can't play.

Gg

Hh

Hh is for house,
huge, and humongous.
Happy humans love it.
They always help and hug us.

Honeybees love honey.
Horses love hay.
Hares love carrots
on a hot, humid day.

Hh

Ii

Ii makes 2 sounds:
ĭ and ī,
ĭ for igloo
ī for ice.

Ĭ for sit, icky,
and hit.
Ī for hi! I like pie.

Ii

Jj

Jj is for jumping jacks,
jelly, and jam.
Jj is for juice
I enjoy with my ham.

Jj is for jellyfish,
Jupiter, and jet.
Jj is for jaguar,
It's not a good pet.

Jj

Kk

Kk is for keyboard,
kettledrum, and kazoo.
These are cool instruments
I love to play too.

K is for karate.
Be a king for a day.
K is for kite
and Kwanzaa, the holiday.

Ll

Ll is for lollipop,
letter, and log.
Ll is for Labrador,
a really cool dog.

Ll is for lion
and leopard too.
Ll is for ladybug,
crawling on my shoe.

Mm

Mm is for money.
Mommy takes me to the mall.
Mm is for macaroni
and a mighty meatball.

Mm is for monkey
swinging from a tree.
Mm is for magic,
magician, and me.

Nn

Nn is for neighbor,
and a nice, new nurse.
Nn is for our nation.
The Native Americans were here first.

Nn is for nametag
and hot noodle soup.
Nn is for nightingales
nesting in a group.

Nn

Oo

Oo makes 2 sounds:
ŏ and ō,
ŏ for ostrich
ō for ocean.

Ŏ for octagon,
stop, and mop.
Ō for oak,
smoke, and choke.

Pp

Pp is for peanuts,
popcorn, and pie.
Pp is for my pink purse.
I love to shop and buy.

Pp is for penny,
pizza, and pears.
Pp is for people
saying a prayer.

Qq

Qq is for quarter,
question mark, and quack.
Qq is for quartet
singing back to back.

Qq is for quilt,
quiet, and queen.
Qq is for quadruplets
eating ice cream.

Rr

Rr is for rabbit
hopping round and round.
Rr is for radio
rock 'n' roll sounds.

Rr is for rollerblading
and rafting on a river.
Rr is for a roast beef
and ravioli dinner.

Rr

Ss

Ss is for sandwich
and sipping on soup.
Ss is for silly socks
and snakes in a group.

Ss is for soccer,
my sister screams loud.
Ss is for summer sun
sneaking through the clouds.

Ss

Tt

Tt is for television,
turtle, and two.
Tt is for tiger
living in a zoo.

Tt is for telephone,
Tara called Tim.
Tt is for T-rex
with a ferocious grin.

Uu

Uu makes 2 sounds:
ŭ and ū,
ŭ for umbrella,
ū for ukulele.

Ŭ for uncle,
unbutton, and cup.
Ū for unicorn
and Uranus way up.

Vv

Vv is for victory,
let's vote for him!
Vv is for vegetables
and violin.

Vv is for vacuum,
vowels, and vines.
Vv is for volcano
and valentine.

Ww

Ww is for watermelon,
warm and sweet.
Big whales waltz
to the waves and the beat.

Ww is for water rides,
wet, and fun.
Ww is for weather,
we welcome each one.

Xx

Xx is for x-ray.
I spy bones.
Xx is for Xmas
and xylophone.

Xx is for Xavier,
a really special name.
X marks the spot
on maps and games.

Yy

Yy is for yo-yo,
yellow, and year.
Yy is for yacht,
and a yak yelling near.

Yy is for "Yes!"
"Yippy!" and "Yahoo!"
Yy is for yummy
or yucky yam stew.

Zz

Zz is for zebra.
I've seen quite a few.
Zz is for zipper
and zigzag too.

Zz is for zero
Zz is for zest!
Zz is for zither,
an instrument I like best.

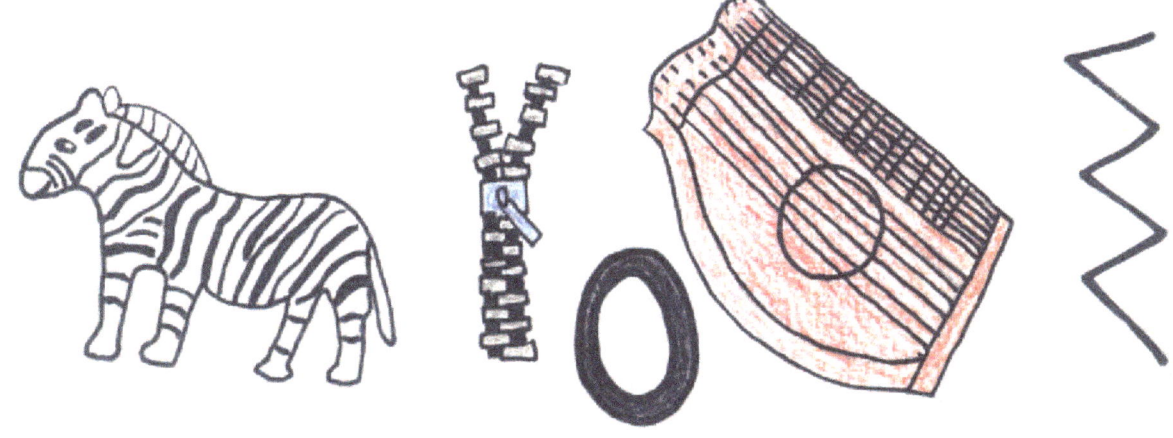

Colors

COLORS

More than just the rainbow.
All colors in the world
are displayed so wonderfully
on every man, woman, boy, and girl.

Colors are in our environment.
They show their beauty again and again.
You ask me what's my favorite color,
I don't know where to begin.

I like all colors in different ways.
I guess I have the COLOR CRAZE!

Red

Red, red
R-E-D.
Red is an apple
delicious as can be.

Red is a fire engine
rolling down the street.
Red is a stop sign.
Rest your feet.

Orange

O-R-A-N-G-E,
Orange is the pumpkin
as big as can be.

Orange is a sunset.
Orange is a fruit.
Orange is the color
of a round fruit loop.

Yellow

Y-E-L-L-O-W,
The big, yellow bus
is passing through.

Bananas, soup,
a big yellow sun.
Yellow is a duck
and butter on a bun.

Green

Green, green
lima beans.
Grass and plants
and spinach cuisine.

G-R-E-E-N,
Green is the color
of a space alien.

Blue

B-L-U-E,
Blue is an ocean
as wide as can be.

Blue is a blue jay.
Blue is the sky.
Blue are the blueberries
in a pie.

Purple

P-U-R-P-L-E,
Purple is a lilac
as pretty as can be.

Purple is a violet
growing in the sun.
Purple is the color
of a ripe, tasty plum.
Yum, yum!

 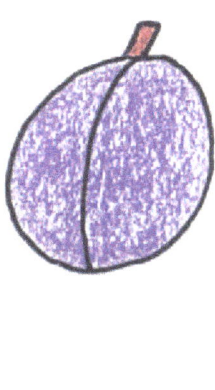

Black

B-L-A-C-K,
Black is darkness
I can't find my way.

Black is a pencil point.
Black is the street.
Black is a black bear
with really large feet.

White

W-H-I-T-E,
White is the snow
as we go to ski.

White is a cloud
way up in the sky.
White is an airplane
flying so high.

Brown

B-R-O-W-N,
Brown is the color
of a violin.

Brown is a graham cracker.
Brown is dirt.
Brown is a messy stain
on my shirt.

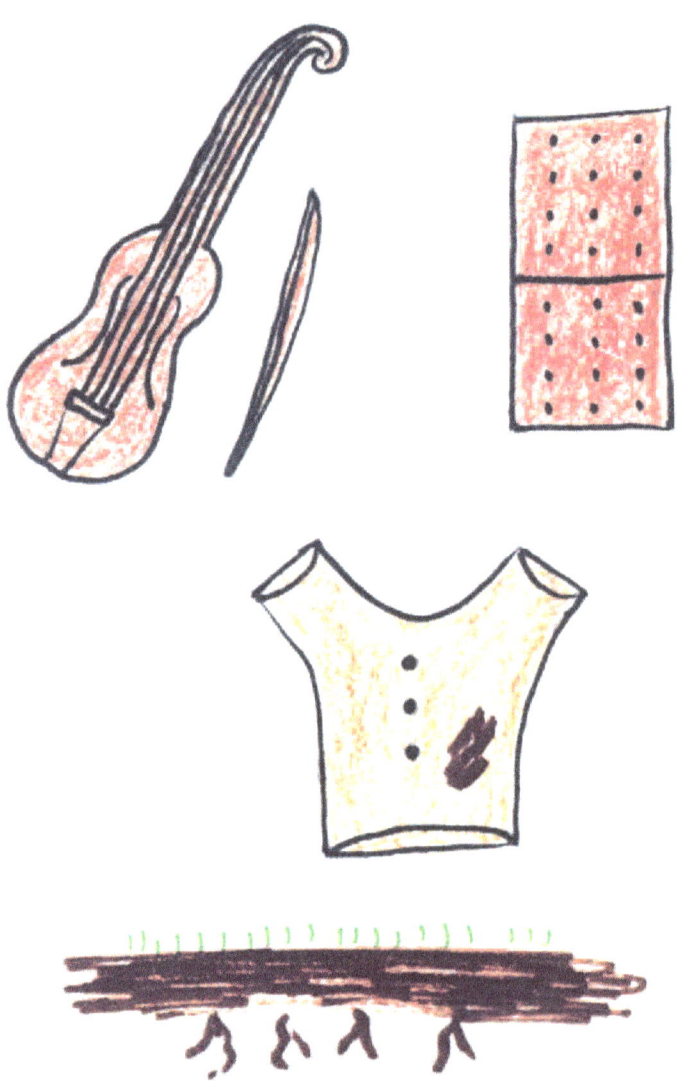

Pink

P-I-N-K,
Pink is a pig
and a beautiful bouquet.

Pink is my tongue
inside my mouth.
Pink is a pretty napkin
at a cookout.

Gray

G-R-A-Y,
Gray is an antenna
on a roof up high.

Gray is an elephant.
Gray is a mouse.
Gray is a metal fence
around my house.

Tan

Tan, tan,
T-A-N.
It's lighter than brown,
and the color of sand.

Tan is a piece of wood
And wooden beads.
Tan is a clothes pin
And different kinds of seeds.

Gold

Gold, gold,
G-O-L-D.
A darker shade of yellow,
wouldn't you agree?

Gold is a goldfish
in a bowl.
A leprechaun has a pot of gold
as I've been told.

Lavender

L-A-V-E-N-D-E-R,
Lavender is a flower
we can smell near or far.

A lighter shade of purple,
we see in summer and spring.
Lavender is the unique color
of many pretty things.

Numbers

NUMBERS

Numbers, numbers
everywhere.
We see them single.
We see them in pairs.

We see so many numbers
connected with signs.
We see them with shapes.
We see them with lines.

We make groups of numbers
and count them 1, 2, 3.
Numbers are a big part
of our society.

We do math with numbers
and learn all we can.
We learn to write numbers
So now we understand.
NUMBERS ARE SO GRAND!

Zero

Z-E-R-O,
O stands for nothing
I'm sure you know.

Nil, nul, zilch.
A number minus the same
will always equal zero.
Nothing remains.

One

1, 1
O-N-E
It sounds like a "w"
but an "o" we see.

1 little nose
in the middle of my face.
1 smiley mouth
and 1 neck in place.

Two

2, 2
T-W-O
2 ears and 2 eyes
2 players for tic-tac-toe.

2 is a pair.
Opposites come in twos.
2 big feet
and a pair of new shoes.

Three

3, 3
T-H-R-E-E
3 are triplet
chimpanzees.

3 wheels on a tricycle.
A triangle has 3 points and sides.
An alien monster
could have 3 scary eyes.

Four

4, 4
F-O-U-R
4 black wheels
on any kind of car.

A square has 4 sides
with 4 points too.
4 is a quartet
and quadruplets, that's true.

Five

5, 5

F-I-V-E

A pentagon has 5 points and sides
as we can see.

5 is a nickel
and a 5 dollar bill.
5 pretty flowers
on a windowsill.

Six

6, 6
S-I-X
6 silly socks
and 6 insects.

A group of sextuplets
strolling down the street.
A hexagon has 6 sides
and points that meet.

Seven

7, 7
S-E-V-E-N
7 is a number
that's 3 less than 10.

7-11 is a popular store.
7 rhymes with heaven
but not much more.

10−3=7

Eight

8, 8
E-I-G-H-T
8 long arms
on an octopus in the sea.

An octagon has 8 points
and 8 sides too.
A spider has 8 legs
they love to crawl on you.

Nine

9, 9
N-I-N-E
9 is an odd number
6 + 3.

A cat has 9 lives
that's what people say.
10 - 1 = 9
Math is okay.

6+3

9

10-1=9

Ten

10, 10

T-E-N

10 toes and fingers
we can count all of them.

10 numbers in a phone number
with area code also.
A dime equals 10 cents.
Ten dollars is a lot of dough.

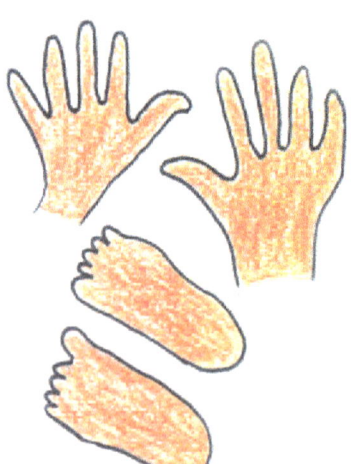

10

(000) 593-0000

About the Author

Linda Taylor has molded kids' lives as a teacher for more than 25 years. She uses her poetry, songs, and chants in her kindergarten classroom to enhance learning and motivate her students. Linda holds an M.S. degree in Education from C.U.N.Y. at City College. She's the author of the AMAZING ANNABELLE series, which has eleven chapter books. Linda is also the author of the DARING DAVID chapter book series, which consists of 11 books. She lives with her family in Long Island, NY.

She has also authored three other poetry books:

        REALLY COOL ANIMAL POEMS

        POEMS THROUGHOUT THE YEAR AND BEYOND

        POETRY RHYMES FOR THE HEART, SOUL, AND MIND

www.ingramcontent.com/pod-product-compliance
Lightning Source LLC
Chambersburg PA
CBHW081757100526
44592CB00015B/2465